OTHER TITLES BY DOUG WARHIT

BOOK THE JOB
(143 Things Actors Need To Know
To Make It Happen)

WARHIT'S GUIDEBOOK FOR THE ACTOR

49 SCENES WITH BITE:
(Pieces Actors Can Sink Their Teeth Into)

AF208026

The above titles may be purchased in bulk
at special discount rates by contacting:

Dau Publishing
10650 Holman Ave. Suite 205
Los Angeles Ca 90024
PHONE: (310) 560-8474
FAX: (310) 446-4815
Email: Daupub@aol.com

TABLE OF CONTENTS

THE
ACTOR'S
AUDITION
CHECKLIST

DOUG WARHIT
ACTING COACH

Dau Publishing
Los Angeles, California

Dau Publishing
10650 Holman Ave. Suite 205
Los Angeles Ca. 90024

Editor: Gladys Itkin & Dawn Herriott
Cover Design & Layout: Declan Geraghty

Publisher's Cataloging-in-Publication Data

Warhit, Doug
        The actor's audition checklist/Doug Warhit
        p. cm.
        ISBN 0-9726262-8-X
        1. Acting-Auditions. 1. Title.
    PN2071.A92 2003
    792'.028-dc21   03-101124
                                                              CIP

Printed in the United States of America

CHAPTER 1

BEFORE YOU WALK THROUGH THE DOOR

It's your audition.
You lead, they follow.

Don't wait for
permission to have a
good time.

It's not you against "them." You're both here in service of the story.

Your acting career will never come down to a single audition.

Make the assumption you're the one they've been looking for.

Your primary focus of attention must be on what your character is fighting for, not the approval of the casting people.

What is the one thing you can bring to this role that no one else in the world can?....

yourself.

Holding back on an audition is like deciding you can't have fun on a date because you're not married yet.

Decide you're going to have a great time and you'll always please the most important person in the room: you.

Don't wait until you're
hired to show them
what you can really do.

The three cardinal sins
for actors:
being desperate, dull,
and late.

If they keep you waiting, don't let it throw you. It's good practice for when they hire you and you're waiting on the set.

If they keep you waiting, don't lose your focus, get angry, or kill time gossiping with other actors. Use the time to go more deeply into your character's prior and given circumstances.

"*I don't know why my agent even bothered submitting me. That other actor waiting to read is perfect for the role.*"

The good news is you're not the casting director. Stick to your own job. That's more than enough to focus your attention on.

Close your eyes and visualize the audition exactly the way you want it to go. Then imagine your agent calling and saying that you booked the job. Then picture yourself on the set actually doing the job.

Try the following experiment: pretend it's the other person's audition and you're there to make them look good. You'll get your attention off yourself and onto them, where it should be.

If you've done something in the past that helped to create the conditions for you to do your best work, take note of what it was so you can do it every time. That way doing your best won't be an accident, but an expectation.

Never let them catch you acting.

Don't forget to breathe.

Come in prepared to do the performance you're going to deliver when they hire you.

Listening is the fuel that creates the need for your verbal response.

Trust your impulses.

The reason you're given more than one scene to prepare is so you can reveal different facets of your character in each scene.

It takes a great actor to bring mediocre writing to life. That's why they thought of you for the role in the first place.

Some actors say they do their best work when they don't care whether they get the part or not. What they really mean is they care enough to do good work, but not enough to drive themselves crazy worrying about the outcome.

The phrase, "*throwing away your homework*" means, if you've done a good solid preparation, you can trust that the choices you've made are in your body and you don't need to think about them. It doesn't mean you didn't need to make those choices in the first place.

Many actors say to themselves, "*I don't care if I get the job. I only want them to like me*" or "*If I don't embarrass myself, I'll be happy.*"

Well, guess what? If that's all you ask for, that's probably all you'll get.

Blaming the
"bad writing"
is a wonderful excuse,
but it won't get
you the job.

If the word *"audition"*
has a negative
connotation, re-label it a
"fiesta." It will remind
you the whole thing is
supposed to be fun.

Begin your involvement in the life of the character before you even leave home. That way the actual audition will be a continuation of the life you've already created.

Always ask yourself how your wardrobe choices can enhance who your character is and contribute to what she is fighting for.

Your wardrobe should suggest the character. It shouldn't hit the casting people over the head.

Never go to
"an audition."
Imagine instead, you're
going to wherever your
character would
be going.

Auditioning is an
opportunity to play. It's
never a matter of life
and death.

Never make any single audition "the be all, end all" of your career. Number one: it won't help you do your best work. Number two: it's a lie.

CHAPTER 2

TEN ESSENTIAL QUESTIONS

What's taking place in the scene?
(GIVEN CIRCUMSTANCES)

What do I want?
(GOAL/SUPER-OBJECTIVE)

Who and what are keeping me from getting what I want?
(OBSTACLES)

What steps will I take to get what I want?
(ACTIONS/TACTICS/
SUB-OBJECTIVES)

W hat is my relationship to the other characters in the scene?

D o the other characters help or hinder my pursuit of what I want?

How does what happened before the scene impact me?

How does the place where the scene occurs impact me?

What is my secret or hidden agenda?

What statement can I write at the top of each scene and silently repeat three times that will immediately get me involved in the scene?

e.g. *"How can I get you to love me?" "Please don't leave me." "I'm going to hurt you." "How can I trust you?"*

CHAPTER 3

GETTING MORE SPECIFIC

What is the single most important thing your character needs to accomplish?

What is the one thing your character can't live without?

How will your character's life be different if she gets what she's fighting for? If she doesn't get it?

How far is your character willing to go to get what he wants?

Your objective must turn you on and inspire you to action. It must be something you ache to achieve. It can't just be an intellectual choice you make and then forget about.

Your objective must serve the script. It can't be arbitrarily selected.

Always write down your overall objective in large letters at the top of the scene so you can glance at it right before you read.

Once you determine your overall objective, you must figure out the steps you'll take to achieve it. (ACTIONS)

If your overall goal is to punish your enemy, your actions might include: to manipulate, to denigrate, to embarrass, to scold, to patronize, to harass, to torment, to intimidate, to conquer, to deflate, to bait, to bluff, to squash, to ignore, to freeze out, and to trample.

Are the obstacles your character faces internal, external, or both?

Without obstacles, there is no drama. Without obstacles, there is no comedy. Without obstacles, there is no audience.

Who are you?

What is unique about your character?

What are your character's strengths? Weaknesses?

What are five adjectives you can use to describe your character?

Are you the hero? If not, do you help or hinder the hero in the pursuit of what she wants?

Make a list of similarities and differences between yourself and the character. The differences are what you need to personalize.

How does your character speak? Pace/ volume/level of articulation?

How does your character move? Quickly/slowly/ energetically/ lethargically/ confidently/clumsily?

Where is your character from? How does that impact your character right now?

What is your character's Achilles heel? (Weakness/fatal flaw)

What is your character's relationship with money?

Is your character's sexuality a source of pride/power/shame?

What is the one thing your character always carries in her pocket or purse?

Does your character have a sense of humor? What about?

What is your character's relationship to the other characters in the scene? Does she love them? Hate them? Trust them? Tolerate them? Want to obliterate them? Make love to them?

What response or reaction is your character striving to evoke from the other characters in the scene?

Every character operates out of self-interest.

Characters don't always say what they mean. Sometimes they mean more than they're saying and sometimes they mean the opposite (SUBTEXT).

Every character has a strong opinion about everything they say and do.

Does the place where the scene occurs support or interfere with the pursuit of your objective?

CHAPTER 4

IN THE CASTING DIRECTOR'S OFFICE

You're the most important person in the room. That's why you're the center of attention.

If you believe you deserve to be here, they will too.

Enter the room as if you're going to hang out with friends you've known all of your life.

Yes, you're in the casting director's office, but you're also in the place where your character is about to commit murder or the hotel room where you and your lover secretly rendezvous.

"I just got the sides. I got stuck in traffic. My agent sent me the wrong material."

If you make excuses at the audition, they will assume you'll make excuses when you get the job. Save the drama for the role.

Just do the work. Don't complain and don't explain.

A reading is not only a chance to demonstrate how wonderful your work is, but an opportunity to show how easy you are to work with.

If you need a moment to center in front of them, that's fine, but that moment shouldn't take more than five seconds.

Before you begin, take a breath, and make eye contact with the reader.

Commit to your choices. Don't second guess yourself.

The casting director will not take responsibility for your performance. Don't take responsibility for his.

The quality of your work is contingent on your ability, not the reader's. If she gives you something to react to, use it. Otherwise, use your imagination and focus on what she's saying, not how she's saying it.

Don't allow their response or lack of one to determine the caliber of your work. If it's a comedy and they laugh hysterically, that's wonderful. But what if they've already seen the scene fifty times? Or, what if the casting person got into a "fender bender" on the way to work?

If the casting people seem rude or unfriendly, they were that way long before they met you. Remember, you'll be able to leave in a few minutes. They're stuck with themselves forever.

If you know you do your best work after running the scene three or four times, find a way to do so before the audition. It is not the casting director's responsibility to run it with you until you're *"there."*

Your primary connection must be with the person you're reading with, not the piece of paper you're holding.

Let them see your eyes. Don't bury your head in the script.

Think of the sides (audition scenes) as a good friend you are allowed to bring into the casting session with you. You don't have to look at your friend if you don't need to, but he or she is a glance away, just in case.

Turn the pages of each scene as you work, even if you don't think you need to. That way if you forget a line, you can just look down, find your place, and continue.

You're not just acting when you're saying your own lines. You're also acting when you're listening.

Don't kiss, kick, spit on, or even touch the casting director. If he can smell your breath, you're way too close. Spark his interest by connecting emotionally, not physically.

Your scent should not get there before you or stay there after you've left.

Unless you are told otherwise, do not bring props in with you. Making strong choices, connecting, and listening are more than enough to be concerned about.

Actors sometimes think they've ruined the entire reading if they accidentally change a word or fumble a line. Everyone makes mistakes and if you don't make a big deal out of it, neither will they.

Don't pressure yourself to manufacture the emotion you think you're supposed to be feeling. Keep your focus on fighting for what your character needs.

If you rush, you communicate that you value the casting director's time more than your own and that you don't deserve to be here.

A directorial adjustment is a positive sign. It means they're responding to something you're already bringing to the role.

If you're not clear on their direction, ask for clarification. It won't help to nod your head in understanding if you're confused.

If your pattern is to think of everything you should have done after the reading is over, do a stronger preparation and spend more time on relaxation.

If you get a callback it means what you did at the first reading worked. Unless you are told otherwise, stick to the choices that got you there.

CHAPTER 5

EXPECTING THE UNEXPECTED

When you're dealing with casting people (and any other human beings) something unexpected always happens. You must be flexible and adapt quickly. Maintain a sense of humor and try not to take it personally.

The following are some of the things that might happen:

Your agent said you were just reading for the casting director, but when you get in the room there are four producers, three writers, and the director waiting to see your work. Take a deep breath and focus on your character's objective.

You were told you were reading with Tom Hanks, but when you get in the room, only the casting director's assistant is there. Take a deep breath and focus on your character's objective.

You get completely new pages when you arrive. If you need some time to prepare, it's your responsibility to ask for it.

You were told to prepare all five scenes, but now they're only doing scenes one and four. Your preparation should include running the audition material in various sequences until it doesn't matter which scenes you're asked to do, or in which order you're asked to do them.

You've rehearsed standing, but when you get in the room they direct you to sit. From now on, rehearse standing and sitting. That way you'll be comfortable either way.

They decide you aren't physically right for the part so they give you the sides for another character. Take the time you need to prepare in the waiting room.

They tape your audition after you were told they wouldn't be taping it.
Keep your focus on the reader, not the camera (unless you're told otherwise).

The casting director reads one of your lines by mistake. Don't blame him. Just say *"I think we switched lines. Can we take it back a couple of lines."*

The casting director is reading all of the other roles in the scene and decides to skip down and just give you your cue line. If you're thrown, politely ask to take it back a couple of lines.

The phone rings and the producer leaves to take an emergency call in the middle of your reading. If you're thrown, politely tell them you'd like to start over.

They eat lunch while you're reading. Keep your focus on what your character is fighting for.

Use the unexpected as an opportunity to make your work even more spontaneous.

CHAPTER 6

PRE-AUDITION JITTERS

Focus on your breathing. With each exhalation silently repeat the word "*relax*." Notice where in your body you're feeling tense. Tighten that area as much as you can. Then relax. Then tighten. Then relax.

Get your attention off yourself. Focus on an object (a lamp, a painting, a desk, your hand) in the waiting room. Study this object until you can close your eyes and recall every detail.

Carry a small rubber ball with you. Squeeze it as hard as you can. Imagine you are transferring every ounce of your anxiety onto the ball.

Imagine the place where the scene occurs. Be very specific. Use as many of your five senses as possible.

Bring a walkman with you and listen to music that puts you in the mood of your character.

Do some push-ups and some jumping jacks before you get to the audition. Run around the block. You'll get out of your head and into your body.

Stand with your knees slightly bent. Slowly bend your upper torso toward the ground. Go as far over as you can without straining your back. Stay there with your head bent toward the ground and slowly count to ten. Then raise your upper body one vertebrae at a time until you are standing up as straight as you can.

Go to the restroom. Make funny faces at yourself in the mirror. Stick your tongue out, put one thumb in your ear and the other in your nose and wave at yourself with your eight remaining fingers. Speak to yourself in gibberish.

Go to the restroom. Pretend you're a monkey. Jump up and down, scratch and make monkey sounds (quietly). Congratulations! You've just made a monkey out of yourself. Now you don't have to worry about anyone else doing it.

Imagine the people you are reading for sitting on toilets doing their business.

Imagine the people you are reading for are ducks: quacking, pooping, and waddling around.

When you enter the audition room, in addition to seeing the casting people, imagine a good friend or a family member or an inspiring teacher is also there to greet you. Hear him say, *"You're the greatest!"* *"Relax and just have fun."* *"I know you can do it."*

CHAPTER 7

COMMERCIALS

The slate (saying your name directly to the camera, before reading the copy) is your mini-commercial. Don't rush it.

Allow your slate to communicate that you're happy to be there and ready to play.

Imagine you're speaking to someone you care about, rather than just a camera lens.

If you're supposed to be turned on by the product but you're not, imagine something else that does genuinely excite you.

Don't judge yourself, the product, or the copy. Immerse yourself in the given circumstances, no matter how ridiculous they may appear to the outside world.

Your non-verbal reactions are at least as important as any dialogue you have.

If you flub a line or change a word, don't apologize or make a big deal out of it. It's not important that you get every word right, only that you have fun.

Doing commercials is not about being phony. It's about being genuine. Create a sense of reality and believability for everything you say and do.

CHAPTER 8

One-liners

Approach one-liners with the same degree of enthusiasm and specificity as you would for larger roles. Create a strong sense of place, a specific moment before, and an objective appropriate to the material.

Relax. You don't need to hit them over the head with your choices or to steal focus from the main characters.

Be prepared to play your part with three distinct interpretations.

If you're not clear on what they're looking for, ask.

Your focus of attention should be on the reader, not listening to how you sound.

Reading for one or two liners is an opportunity to make a positive impression on the same people who can bring you in to read for larger roles in the future.

CHAPTER 9

AUDITION AFFIRMATIONS

Slowly repeat each affirmation three times:

I deserve to be here and I'm ready to play.

I relish the chance to show them what I can do.

I rise to the challenge and I give 100%.

No one can bring as much to this role as I can.

I allow myself to do the work I know I am capable of.

I trust the choices I've made and I have no need to push the emotion or force the results.

I know that I'm talented and this audition is merely one of many opportunities I'll be having over the course of my long, successful career.

Although their focus of attention is on me, my focus is on what my character is fighting for.

I'm in it for the long haul. Therefore, I will never allow any single audition to become a matter of life and death.

My work is truthful, specific, and exciting.

I bring more to the role than even the director envisioned.

I let go of my need for control.

I let go of my need for approval.

I trust my impulses.

I really listen.

The choices I've made
are in my body and I
allow them to manifest
fully.

Now create three empowering affirmations of your own:

1.

2.

3.

DOUG WARHIT

Doug Warhit has been teaching on-camera cold reading and scene study classes in Los Angeles to beginners through working professionals for over twenty years. He is also a licensed psychotherapist, specializing in actors' issues of self-sabotage, performance anxiety, and procrastination.

FOR INFORMATION ON PRIVATE AND GROUP ON-CAMERA CLASSES & ONE DAY AND WEEKEND INTENSIVES IN THE U.S. AND CANADA

Contact:
Doug Warhit at (310) 479-5647.
Or visit his website:
www.dougwarhit.com